Introduction

Much attention has been given in the financial press to the sharp declines that took place since 1995 in the spreads paid by emerging market countries on their debt over yields on bonds issued by industrial country governments. By mid-1997, spreads on Brady bonds had plunged to levels which obtained in early 1994, before the Mexican financial crisis caused yields to soar. Concerns were raised that credit spreads on emerging market debt instruments might have fallen too far, and were below levels that adequately covered risk.

> "Serious financial institutions are buying billions of dollars of long-term bonds from countries that five years ago were regarded as economic disaster areas. Moreover, they have been buying them at razor-thin margins over US Treasury bond yields."
>
> (Financial Times, 10 July 1997)

The advent of the Asian financial crisis in the second half of 1997 has been viewed as confirming suspicions that spreads had fallen too low to cover risk, but it remains unclear as to why spreads declined as much as they did. Various factors have been cited for the declines in spreads on emerging market bonds. First, it has been suggested that the declines represented, in part, the resumption of a longer-term trend toward reduced credit spreads that was interrupted by the Mexican financial crisis. This trend may have reflected improvements in the creditworthiness of emerging market borrowers, particularly in Latin America, where many countries have implemented programs of stabilisation and structural reform. It may also have reflected a process of what is loosely referred to as "globalisation," that is, an increasing willingness of industrial country investors to lend to emerging market countries on the same basis as to industrial country borrowers. This process of globalisation may be associated with increased knowledge about and experience with emerging market borrowers, as well as with an increased desire among industrial country borrowers to achieve gains through international portfolio diversification.

While market commentary acknowledges the importance of these factors in the trend decline in emerging market credit spreads, considerably greater weight has been placed on another factor: the low level of industrial country short-term interest rates. It is argued that these low rates increased the demand for riskier investments, including emerging market debt, in order to support high rates of return on investment portfolios.

> "...central banks in Japan and continental Europe are still pursuing an expansionary monetary policy, pushing money into their economies in an attempt to revive the spirits of consumers...This excess liquidity has spilled over into financial assets on a global basis, driving up prices. Much of the money ends up in the hands of investors in the US which scour the world in search of higher returns." (Financial Times, 10 July 1997)

> "There is a big demand for spread because we are in another era of high global liquidity and low interest rates," says Sylvia Maxfield, sovereign analyst at Lehmann Brothers Inc. in New York. (Wall Street Journal, 6 May 1997)

If credit spreads on emerging market debt instruments genuinely are influenced by industrial country short-term interest rates, this has important implications for policymakers. First, it implies that spreads are being determined by factors other than creditworthiness alone and that high levels of global liquidity could lead spreads to fall below levels that adequately cover risk, as may have occurred prior to the Asian financial crisis. Secondly, a high sensitivity of spreads to the level of industrial country interest rates means that in the event of an upturn in these rates, the cost of financing to emerging market countries will rise by an even greater extent, posing a further threat to balance-of-payments positions.

However, notwithstanding the large volume of market commentary, there has been little formal statistical analysis to substantiate the claim that low industrial country interest rates, presumably reflecting increased global liquidity, were responsible for declines in emerging market bond spreads. It is possible that these declines may have been caused by other factors, such as the dissipation of the impact of the Mexican financial crisis, combined with the longer term effects of improved creditworthiness and globalisation of international financial markets.

Moreover, much of the market commentary on declines in spreads has been based on trends in the most commonly used gauge of emerging market bond spreads, Brady bond spreads, even though these spreads may not be representative of the financing costs paid by a broad range of emerging market country borrowers. Brady bonds represent restructured commercial bank debt of governments that faced difficulties repaying their obligations during the debt crisis of the 1980s. Both the level and movements of Brady bond spreads differ significantly from those on the bonds issued by many other emerging market borrowers. Nevertheless, most market observers have focused on Brady bond spreads, in large part because of the widespread availability of this measure.

In this paper, we describe research designed to address two related issues. First, we attempt to develop a more complete picture of the evolution of emerging market credit spreads during the 1990s, up until the Asian financial crisis, than that provided by Brady bond spreads alone. Using a database of new bond and loan issues from emerging market countries, we are able to identify trends in credit spreads while controlling for other important determinants of spreads, including creditworthiness, maturity, currency denomination, and region of issue.

Our analysis confirms suspicions that emerging market spreads in the years preceding the Asian financial crisis declined by more than can be explained by improvements in risk factors alone. While this result is echoed by other recent analyses of non-Brady bond data (see Cline and Barnes (1997) and Eichengreen and Mody (1998a), a key contribution of our research is that it identifies different trends in spreads for emerging market debt instruments with different levels of creditworthiness. We discovered that while spreads on the riskiest credits behaved much like Brady bond spreads, rising with the Mexican financial crisis and declining thereafter, spreads on investment grade credits to emerging market countries exhibited a very different pattern, declining steadily throughout the 1992-97 period and enjoying the benefits of a "flight to quality" during the period of the Mexican crisis.

Our ability to distinguish among different trends in spreads was facilitated by our use of commercial credit ratings as a measure of creditworthiness instead of the collection of indicators, such as debt/GDP, reserves/imports, etc., more commonly used to gauge credit risk. Our approach makes it straightforward to calculate standard, aggregative measures of emerging market credit spreads for different ratings classifications, and also lends itself to use by market participants evaluating prospective market spreads for future issues of given ratings and maturity.

The second objective of this paper is to cast some light on the factors responsible for the evolution over time of emerging market credit spreads. In particular, we attempt to evaluate the relative contributions of longer term trends in credit spreads, of the Mexican financial crisis, and of variations in industrial country interest rates. In contrast to the implications of much financial market commentary, we find little role for industrial country interest rates in the determination of spreads on emerging market bonds. This result holds both for the new issue spreads described above, after controlling for movements in credit quality, maturity, and other attributes, as well as for Brady bond spreads.

The plan of the paper is as follows. In Section 1, we review various measures of emerging market credit spreads and discuss problems with these data. We then discuss measures of emerging market credit spreads derived from data contained in the Capital DATA Bondware and Loanware databases. In Section 2, we present and estimate a regression equation that controls for creditworthiness, maturity, and other attributes, thereby allowing underlying trends in spreads to be identified. Section 3 adds measures of industrial country interest rates to the model in order to evaluate the hypothesis that declines in industrial country rates are responsible for the recent declines in emerging market credit spreads. The section also puts these results into perspective by examining the behaviour of Brady bond spreads and by summarising the results of some related studies. Section 4 concludes.

1. Measures of emerging market credit spreads

The analysis in this paper is restricted to debt instruments, bonds and loans, issued by emerging market countries that are denominated in a major industrial country currency, mainly dollars, yen, and Deutsche marks. Spreads are defined as the (promised) annualised yield on the emerging market debt instrument less the benchmark yield, the annualised yield on an industrial country government bond of the same currency denomination and maturity as the emerging market instrument.[1]

As noted above, the most widely cited measure of spreads on emerging market debt instruments are stripped spreads on Brady bonds.[2] Chart 1 shows the J P Morgan measure of weighted average stripped spreads on Brady bonds in the secondary market for ten emerging market countries: Argentina, Brazil, Bulgaria, Ecuador, Mexico, Nigeria, Panama, Peru, Poland and Venezuela.[3] Brady bond spreads are available on a high-frequency basis, which partially accounts for why they have been the main focus of market attention to date. In addition, the market for Brady bonds has been deeper and more active than markets for other emerging market country obligations, which suggests that their prices may be a more reliable measure of underlying asset values.[4] For these reasons, spreads on Brady bonds have been of much interest to market observers and participants.

However, the surge in bank borrowing and (non-Brady bond) securities issuance by emerging market countries during the 1990s, at least prior to the Asian crisis, calls into question the relevance of Brady bond spreads as a general measure of the financing costs paid by these borrowers. Many of the emerging market countries currently issuing bonds had better credit ratings

---

[1] More formally, Spread = $i - ibm$, where i is the annualised yield on emerging market debt instrument and ibm is the annualised yield on an industrial country government bond of the same currency and maturity. For floating rate loans, spreads are measured over six-month or one-year Libor.

[2] The principle and interest on Brady bonds are partially collateralised. Stripped spreads refer to spreads on these bonds, once the estimated effect of the collateral on these spreads is removed.

[3] Spreads are weighted by US dollar amounts.

[4] In fact, at the beginning of the 1990s, Brady bonds were virtually the only longer-term sovereign bonds issued by emerging market countries.

than the countries that issued Brady bonds and hence were charged lower credit spreads.[5] Furthermore, the countries that initially issued Brady bonds are now issuing non-collateralised debt at spreads which frequently are lower than those on outstanding Brady bonds. This may reflect the fact that there was a lesser demand by the market for the security provided by collateralisation, and hence a disinclination to pay for the higher transactions costs associated with that added complexity; additionally, Brady bonds may be viewed as a junior to more recently issued debt.[6]

For all these reasons, trends in Brady bond spreads may not provide an accurate indication of more general movements in emerging market credit spreads. It therefore would be useful if a measure of average spreads on a more representative sample of credits were available.

---

[5] These lower spreads may also reflect the fact that most emerging market instruments have been issued at shorter maturities than Brady bonds, which typically have terms of more than 10 years.

[6] Moreover, to the extent that investors in the secondary market for Bradies and in the primary market for non-collateralised issues differ, this also may lead Brady bond spreads to be unrepresentative of emerging market debt costs more generally.

To the best of our knowledge, however, there exists no readily available alternative to Brady bond-based measures of average emerging market country spreads that accurately and succinctly reflects the borrowing costs paid by the full range of emerging market borrowers.[7] In order to create such an alternate measure, we exploited the Capital DATA Bondware and Loanware databases. These databases provide information on new international bond and loan issues, including the nationality of issuer, amount of loan, maturity, promised yield to maturity and credit rating.[8] In many instances, the information provided also includes the spread over the appropriate industrial country benchmark yield. In contrast to Brady bond spreads, which are based on secondary market prices, the spreads reported in the Capital DATA databases represent actual borrowing costs for emerging market countries.

Based on these data, we calculated weighted (by US dollar amount) average spreads on new issues of bonds and loans by emerging market countries up until mid-1997. (Data on bonds are available from 1991, and on loans from 1992.) These computed spreads are shown in Chart 1 and reveal important differences between spreads on Brady bonds and on emerging market instruments more generally. Most importantly, spreads on Brady bonds have been considerably higher than on other emerging market instruments, probably reflecting a combination of the factors described above: Brady bonds were issued by particularly high-risk countries; they have exceptionally long maturities; the additional complexity associated with the collateralisation may be unwanted by investors; they may be perceived to be junior to other types of instruments; and they may be purchased by different sorts of investors. These considerations make a strong case for

---

[7] Several analysts, including Clark (1994), Andrews and Ishii (1995), IMF (1997) and Cline and Barnes (1997), have examined spreads on selected emerging market Eurobonds as an alternative to Brady bonds, but have not developed a more general index or average based on these spreads. J P Morgan calculates a measure of returns on emerging market bonds, known as EMBI+, that includes Eurobonds as well as Brady bonds. However, the composition of the EMBI+ index remains heavily tilted toward Brady bonds and other instruments issued by Brady bond countries. Finally, Andrews and Ishii (1995), IMF (1997) and Eichengreen and Mody (1998a), among others, present data on average spreads on new emerging market bond issues; however, as will be discussed below, movements in average new issue spreads can be misleading if this measure is not corrected for changes in the composition of new issues.

[8] Credit ratings are those of either Moody's or Standard & Poor's, the two main commercial ratings agencies.

questioning the relevance of Brady bond spreads as a broad indicator of the cost of financing for all emerging market countries.

Notwithstanding these drawbacks to Brady bond spreads, Chart 1 also makes clear that the weighted-average spreads on new bonds and loans that we have calculated exhibit some peculiar patterns over time. For example, the series of average bond spreads declines in the first quarter of 1995, when the Mexican financial crisis occurred and Brady bond spreads peaked, and rises through the remainder of 1995 and early 1996, when the effects of the Mexican financial crisis began to dissipate and Brady bond spreads declined. In contrast, the series on average loan spreads shows virtually no movement at all during the 1990s, notwithstanding an abundance of commentary pointing to declines in spreads on emerging market debt.

These unusual features of the evolution of average spreads probably reflect important changes over time in the composition of new bond and loan issues.[9] In the course of the 1990s, at least prior to the Asian crisis, investors have been prepared to lend at longer maturities as the perceived creditworthiness of emerging market countries has improved, and emerging market countries have willingly paid higher spreads in order to lengthen the maturity structure of their debt. As indicated in Chart 2, average maturities for bonds increased from six years in 1991 to ten years in early 1997, and this has led to a smaller decline in average spreads than otherwise would have occurred. In contrast, average maturities for new loans, which include occasional large long-term project loans, have displayed no long-term trend in the 1990s.

---

[9] The importance of compositional changes in the issuance of securities also is underscored in Andrews and Ishii (1995), Eichengreen and Mody (1998a) and IMF (1997).

Even more important than variations in maturity have been variations in the composition of emerging market borrowers by creditworthiness. Chart 3 indicates the breakdown of new bonds issued by their credit rating. While the share of less creditworthy borrowers in total issuance has not shown any long-term trend, there have been marked year-to-year variations. In particular, the fraction of riskier borrowers in the total dropped off sharply in 1995, when investors responded to the Mexican financial crisis by temporarily cutting off funding to many emerging market economies. Therefore, the plunge in average bond spreads in early 1995 most likely reflects the withdrawal from the market of the most poorly rated borrowers, who pay the highest spreads.

These considerations suggest that, in order to identify underlying movements of credit spreads with our data, maturity and creditworthiness must be taken into account.[10] In principle, this could be accomplished by examining movements over time in very narrowly defined credit categories, for example, BB rated bonds of 10 years maturity. However, as indicated in Table 1, even though our database includes a very large number of bonds and loans, there are at times relatively few observations (for any given category). Hence, directly tracking spreads over time on instruments with particular attributes is not feasible with these data.

---

[10] Implicitly, this is accomplished by examining Brady bond spreads. However, to the extent that these spreads are not representative of emerging market spreads more generally, their movements over time may also be misleading. Additionally, ratings of some of the countries issuing Brady bonds may change over time as their macroeconomic situations and creditworthiness change.

In the following section, we describe an alternative approach in which we estimate a regression equation that relates the spread on emerging market issues to various characteristics of those instruments, including maturity and credit rating. Based on this regression, variations over time in credit spreads that are not explained by movements in maturity, credit ratings, and other factors are then interpreted as the underlying movements in credit spreads.

Table 1

Bond spreads for developing country issuers, by rating and completion quarter

Rating	Spreads (in basis points)				US dollar amounts (in millions)				Number of observations			
	B	BB	BBB	A	B	BB	BBB	A	B	BB	BBB	A
9101		320				125				1		
9103		255				350				3		
9104		314				677				4		
9201	450				90				1			
9202	365	275			100	100			1	1		
9203	525	310			100	400			1	2		
9204	525	419		115	40	740		300	1	4		1
9301		321				1,264				5		
9302	603	339	254	115	230	622	600	1,440	2	6	3	5
9303		252	144	92		1,856	400	488		8	2	2
9304	306	285	151	83	1,668	2,895	350	2,105	6	13	3	5
9401		192	100			2,034	1,750			4	4	
9402		311		89		357		600		2		1
9403		326	138	99		450	100	600		2	1	2
9404	371	391	140	99	992	1,050	200	597	13	4	1	2
9501		232	73	79		67	203	637		1	1	2
9502	375	251		47	50	1,048		491	1	4		2
9503	377	313	110	83	1,624	1,805	1,146	1,500	5	6	4	4
9504	478	424	181	96	1,018	1,287	746	550	8	5	5	2
9601	446	433	178	128	1,310	3,278	1,000	780	4	5	5	3
9602	454	463	151	81	1,574	3,649	770	1,921	9	9	4	7
9603	375	384	173	65	675	2,791	1,049	1,537	6	7	6	7
9604	393	307		56	2,626	3,398		3,384	11	8		9
9701	259	309	119	41	1,175	6,804	1,905	2,148	6	11	5	5
9702	189	226		68	643	585		2,168	4	2		7

2. Regression-based measures of emerging market credit spreads

Table 2 presents the results of estimating regression equations that explain the spread over benchmark yields on emerging market debt instruments. The observations are comprised of 662 new issues, 304 bonds and 358 loans, for which data on both spreads and credit ratings were available, dating from 1991 through to the first half of 1997. Each observation in the regression equations represents a single new issue of a bond or a loan. The dependent variable is the log of the spread on that new issue.[11] The explanatory variables capture various attributes of that new issue such as its credit rating, maturity, currency denomination, and the year in which it was issued.

The regressions are distinguished both by the types of instruments included in the set of dependent variables–the first and third equations include both bonds and loans, while the remaining equations include bonds only–and by the types of explanatory variables. The explanatory variables and their coefficients will now be discussed in turn.

2.1 Explanatory variables and parameter estimates

Bond – Dummy. This dummy variable takes on a value of 1 if the new issue is a bond and 0 if it is a loan. The coefficient is positive and highly significant, indicating that even with credit rating and maturity held constant, a bond has a spread that is more than double the size of a spread on a comparable loan.

This differential could reflect various factors. First, banks may have closer customer relationships with borrowers than bondholders, giving them an advantage in monitoring creditworthiness that shows up in lower spreads. Second, because bondholders typically are more

---

[11] In using the log of the spread rather than the level, we follow the methodology used by Cantor and Packer (1996). In various experiments undertaken to assess the robustness of our results, we found that using the log of the spread improved the fit of the equation to a certain extent, but did not substantially alter the qualitative nature of our results.

Table 2
Emerging market spreads over industrial country benchmarks
Dependent variable: log (spread)

	Bonds & loans	Bonds	Bonds & loans	Bonds	Bonds
Intercept	1.67	2.32	1.54	2.21	289.10
	(7.06)	(9.03)	(8.52)	(9.94)	(5.86)
Bond – Dummy	0.75	–	0.75	–	–
	(19.13)	–	(19.34)	–	–
Rating	0.19	0.19	0.14	0.15	0.15
	(7.66)	(6.95)	(7.15)	(5.92)	(6.25)
Rating * Spec Dummy	0.04	0.04	0.04	0.04	0.04
	(6.33)	(4.16)	(6.41)	(4.32)	(4.01)
Log (Term)	0.65	0.65	0.66	0.65	0.68
	(5.54)	(4.87)	(5.74)	(4.98)	(5.23)
Log (Term) * Log (Rating)	–0.22	–0.20	–0.22	–0.20	–0.21
	(–4.30)	(–3.52)	(4.52)	(–3.67)	(–3.94)
DEM – Dummy	–0.07	–0.02	–0.42	–0.29	–0.29
	(–1.13)	(–0.41)	(–1.09)	(–0.25)	(–0.05)
JPY – Dummy	–0.43	–0.30	–0.42	–0.29	–0.29
	(–4.79)	(–2.86)	(–4.72)	(–2.78)	(–2.73)
OTHER – Dummy	–0.31	–0.30	–0.32	–0.30	–0.33
	(–4.25)	(–4.46)	(–4.37)	(–4.62)	(–4.92)
1991 – Dummy	1.61	1.57	1.12	1.08	–
	(0.58)	(0.70)	(5.72)	(5.79)	–
1992 – Dummy	0.90	1.42	1.08	1.02	–
	(3.343)	(2.90)	(7.99)	(6.86)	–
1993 – Dummy	0.95	0.81	1.08	1.20	–
	(4.42)	(3.80)	(8.51)	(7.11)	–
1994 – Dummy	0.87	0.79	0.99	0.91	–
	(3.95)	(3.30)	(7.53)	(6.00)	–
1995 – Dummy	0.21	0.13	0.41	0.42	–
	(0.99)	(0.60)	(6.26)	(5.88)	–
1996 – Dummy	0.17	0.14	0.31	0.29	–
	(0.88)	(0.81)	(5.09)	(4.80)	–
Rating * 1991 – Dummy	–0.10	–0.09	–	–	–
	(–0.42)	(–0.49)	–	–	–
Rating * 1992 – Dummy	–0.04	–0.07	–	–	–
	(–1.54)	(–1.73)	–	–	–
Rating * 1993 – Dummy	–0.05	–0.03	–	–	–
	(–2.21)	(–1.72)	–	–	–
Rating * 1994 – Dummy	–0.05	–0.04	–	–	–
	(–2.24)	(–1.96)	–	–	–
Rating * 1995 – Dummy	0.02	0.03	–	–	–
	(0.97)	(1.47)	–	–	–
Rating * 1996 – Dummy	0.01	0.01	–	–	–
	(0.74)	(0.85)	–	–	–
Rating * Mexico – Dummy	–	–	0.06	0.05	0.06
	–	–	(5.25)	(4.44)	(4.59)
Time trend	–	–	–	–	–0.15
	–	–	–	–	(–5.80)
Mexico	–	–	–	–	–0.34
	–	–	–	–	(–2.21)
Adj. R – Square	0.81	0.82	0.81	0.82	0.82
No. of observations	662	304	662	304	304

t-statistics are in parentheses.

dispersed and harder to organise than banks, banks may have an advantage over bondholders in recovering value in the event of default.[12]

It is worth noting that bonds and loans are very different types of financial instruments. The new bond issues represented in our data have exclusively fixed interest rates, while the loan issues all have interest rates which are at a fixed initial spread over Libor.[13] Additionally, many facets of the credit contract differ substantially between bonds and loans. Finally, as noted above, relations between borrower and lender are very different for bonds and loans.

These considerations, taken together, would suggest that bond and loan spreads behave so differently that it would be inappropriate to analyse them in the same regression equation. Yet, one of the most surprising results of our research is that emerging market bonds and loans appear to differ only in the level of their spreads, not in the response of their spreads to changes in other explanatory variables such as credit rating (denoted "Rating") or maturity (denoted "Term"). This can be seen by comparing estimated coefficients in the equations for both bonds and loans to those for bonds alone; in most cases, the estimated coefficients are very similar, as are adjusted R^2s. In other regressions (not shown) in which the Bond-Dummy was interacted with all of the other explanatory variables in the model, the coefficients on these interaction terms were not (individually) significantly different from zero and the adjusted R^2 did not rise, further suggesting that spreads on bonds and loans differ only by a constant proportion.[14]

---

[12] Additionally, bond spreads are measured as spreads over industrial country benchmark bonds, whereas loan spreads are measured over Libor. Insofar as Libor tends to exceed benchmark yields by a small margin, this also would tend to lower bank loan spreads relative to bonds spreads somewhat, but not by very much.

[13] It is worth noting that, depending on the covenants, the spread on some loans can be changed in response to changes in certain factors, including the financial condition of the borrower. Such covenants, which shift risk from lender to borrower, could also explain the lower spreads on loans.

[14] Most previous analyses of emerging market debt spreads have focused either on bank loans or on bonds, but not both. One exception is the study by Edwards (1986) that compares models for both loan and bond spreads and finds them to differ significantly in certain respects. This may be due to either the different specification employed or the different time period (1976–80).

Based on these results, we consider it appropriate to pool the data on bonds and loans into a single regression equation. However, for readers that remain unconvinced, the second, fourth, and fifth columns of Table 2 present results for equations based on bond data alone.

Rating and *Rating * Spec Dummy*. Most prior analyses of emerging market debt spreads have used various country performance variables, including the debt/GDP ratio, debt service/exports, reserves/imports, etc., as measures of borrower creditworthiness.[15] However, the study by Cantor and Packer (1996) suggests that the credit ratings assigned to sovereign borrowers by Moody's and Standard & Poor's, completely subsume all information contained in country performance measures, and, in fact, add information relative to those measures in explaining sovereign debt spreads.[16] A further advantage of using credit ratings as a measure of creditworthiness is that these credit ratings take into account many attributes that are specific to the issuer, not merely to the issuer's country of origin. Because our database includes issues by both private and public institutions, credit ratings provide a more precise measure of risk than country performance measures alone. Therefore, we use the credit ratings assigned to new loan and bond issues by Moody's and Standard & Poor's as measures of credit risk.

Table 3 presents the concordance between the two measures, and illustrates the conversion of these measures into numerical rankings, with 1 being the best credit risk and 16 the worst. In those cases where ratings assigned by both Standard & Poor's and Moody's were available, these were identical for 58% of the issues and differed by one notch for 36% of the issues. In cases of conflict, the Moody's rating was chosen to dominate because most of the ratings available in the database were derived from this source.

---

[15] See Edwards (1984, 1986), Ozler (1992), Rockerbie (1993), Demirguc-Kunt and Detragiache (1994), Cline and Barnes (1997) and Min (1998). Some exceptions include Feder and Ross (1982), who use an *Institutional Investor* survey of creditworthiness perceptions as a proxy for credit risk, and Eichengreen and Mody (1998a and 8b), who use both country performance measures and *Institutional Investor* ratings to explain spreads.

[16] See also Ammer (1997) and Larrain, Reisen and von Maltzan (1997).

Table 3

Assignment of numerical values to credit ratings

Order	Moody's	S&P
1	Aaa	AAA
2	Aa1	AA+
3	Aa2	AA
4	Aa3	AA–
5	A1	A+
6	A2	A
7	A3	A–
8	Baa1	BBB+
9	Baa2	BBB
10	Baa3	BBB–
11	Ba1	BB+
12	Ba2	BB
13	Ba3	BB–
14	B1	B+
15	B2	B
16	B3	B–

Finally, visual inspection of the data suggested that the curve relating spreads to ratings was steeper for instruments with speculative grade ratings (BB and B, using Standard & Poor's terminology) than for investment grade instruments (AAA, AA, A, and BBB). Therefore, an interaction term was included, Rating * Spec Dummy, that multiplies Rating by a dummy that is 1 for speculative grade issues and 0 otherwise.

The estimation results indicate that spreads and credit ratings (where a higher rating indicates a greater likelihood of default) are positively related and that this sensitivity is higher for speculative grade issues than for investment grade issues. All else equal, our model predicts that a deterioration of credit ratings in the investment grade range by one notch, say, from BBB+ to BBB, leads to an increase in the spread of 21% (that is, a proportionate increase of one-fifth, not an increase of 21% points). A one-notch deterioration in the speculative grade range would lead to a 26% increase in spreads.[17]

Log(Term) and *Log(Term)*Log(Rating)*. The greater the maturity of an instrument, the more likely it is that the creditworthiness of the borrower will change during the life of the instrument. Hence, the maturity of an instrument is an important determinant of the degree of uncertainty about repayment and is therefore related to the spread.[18] This hypothesis is well supported by the statistically significant, positive coefficients on the Log(Term) variable in the estimation results shown in Table 2.

It is plausible to expect that the effect of the term of an instrument on the spread may depend on the initial credit rating of the borrower. In previous regressions (not shown), we allowed for different slopes of the credit yield curve for different ratings, and found these differences to be important. We also found that these differences could be represented parsimoniously by adding an explanatory variable in which the term of the loan is interacted with the credit rating. As shown in Table 2, the coefficient on Log(Term)*Log(Rating) is negative and highly significant. This implies that the higher (worse) the rating, the lower is the estimated responsiveness of the spread to the term of the issue. In the case of an AAA-rated bond, a 10% increase in the term of the bond leads to an estimated 6.5% increase in the spread; for a B rated bond, a 10% increase in term leads only to a 0.5% rise in the spread.

This diminished responsiveness of spread to term as credit ratings deteriorate has been documented for US corporate bonds as well. In fact, Fons (1994) found that for the worst-rated US corporate ("junk") bonds, spreads actually *decline* as term increases. A standard explanation is that for borrowers with the best credit ratings, the passage of time offers only the opportunity for a

---

[17] These results are highly consistent with those estimated by Cantor and Packer (1996), who examined secondary market spreads on 35 sovereign bonds on a single day in 1995. They estimated an elasticity of 0.22, implying that a one-notch deterioration in credit ratings raises spreads by 25%.

[18] Increases in the term of a bond also lead to heightened risks that the general level of interest rates will change, leading to changes in the value of the bond. However, this consideration should not affect the spread of a bond over a benchmark yield, since interest rate risk already is built into the yield on the benchmark bond.

deterioration of credit quality, while very poor credit risks that survive are likely to experience an improvement in their rating.

However, Helwege and Turner (1996) argue that this effect really reflects the endogeneity of issuance among poor-risk borrowers with respect to variations in creditworthiness not captured by ratings. That is, in the event of improvements in creditworthiness (which may not be captured by ratings), poorly rated firms may both enjoy smaller spreads and issue debt at longer maturities, thereby creating the illusion that the spreads of more poorly rated borrowers are less sensitive to term.

Whether the concern raised by Helwege and Turner applies to the findings shown in Table 2 is an open question. One factor that diminishes this concern is the fact that this paper employs the finest possible gradation of credit rating (BB+, BB, and BB–, instead of just BB, for example), thereby better controlling for credit quality.[19]

Currency Dummies. Inspection of the data suggested that spreads on non-dollar-denominated instruments appeared to be systematically lower than those on dollar-denominated instruments. Such differences could be accounted for by the fact that during much of the 1990s, benchmark yields in non-dollar currencies have been lower than comparable US Treasury yields, and as discussed in the next section, this could lower spreads as well. To control for this, separate dummy variables were included that are equal to 1 if the issue is denominated in Deutsche marks, yen, or other non-dollar currency, and otherwise.[20] The non-dollar currency effect is statistically significant for all currencies except the Deutsche mark.

Period Effects. The final explanatory variables included in the regression are those designed to identify changes in spreads–holding ratings, term, and currency denomination

---

[19] Min (1998) finds that even without interacting a maturity variable with a creditworthiness variable, increases in maturity lead to lower spreads. This could reflect the endogeneity of issuance if his model does not capture variations in creditworthiness precisely enough.

[20] Edwards (1986) tests for currency effects in his sample of Eurobonds in the late 1970s and finds no significant effects. Conversely, Demirguc-Kunt and Detragiache (1994) find some evidence of currency effects in spreads on official loans in the 1970s and 1980s.

constant–over time. The first two columns of Table 2 present the most general specification. Separate dummy variables are included for each year, so that if a bond or loan was issued, for example, in 1994, the variable 1994-Dummy takes on a value of 1, while all of the other year dummies take on a value of 0. No dummy variable is specified for 1997, for which data through the middle of that year are used; therefore, the coefficients on the year dummies represent the difference between the log spread in that year and its value in the first half of 1997.

Additionally, the year dummies are interacted with the Rating variable, so that the responsiveness of spreads to ratings is allowed to vary from year to year. Note that the Rating for an AAA instrument is 1, while it is 16 for a B–instrument: to a first approximation, therefore, the separate year dummies capture movements in spreads for the best credit risks, while spreads on the worst risks are determined both by the year dummies and the interaction terms.

The results are quite similar, both for the equation estimated for bonds and loans and that estimated for bonds alone. The coefficients on the separate year dummies show a declining trend from 1992 through 1994 (relative to 1997), a sharp drop in 1995, and slower declines thereafter. (We ignore 1991, which has few observations and insignificant coefficients). The coefficients on the Rating* Year-Dummy variables are negative and often significant during 1992-94, indicating that during these years, the responsiveness of spreads to ratings was lower than in 1997. This changes in 1995, when the coefficients on the interaction terms become positive, indicating in that year, spreads became more responsive to ratings than in 1997.

Our interpretation of these results, which is consistent with much market commentary, is that in 1995 the Mexican financial crisis induced a "flight to quality" among international investors. This is easily seen on Chart 4, which plots model simulations of the spread on dollar-denominated 10-year bonds for different credit ratings.

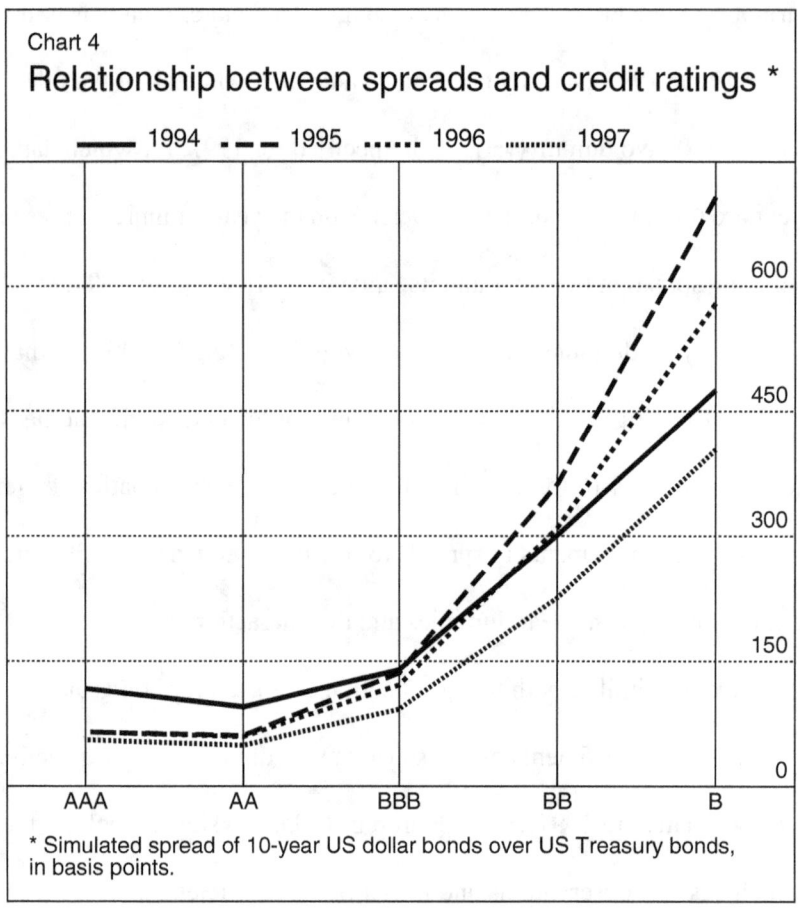

From 1994 to 1995, spreads on the best-rated instruments decline while spreads on the highest-risk borrowers increase, thereby steepening the slope of the curve relating spreads to ratings. Thereafter, spreads on the best-rated instruments decline only slowly, but those on the worst-rated instruments decline more quickly, probably reflecting some dissipation of the effects of the Mexican financial crisis. By the first half of 1997, spreads at all risk levels are below their 1994 levels, suggesting that the effects of the Mexico crisis had largely disappeared. Once more recent data are examined, it will be interesting to see what changes in the spreads-ratings relationship took place later in 1997 and in 1998, as the Asian financial crisis intensified and spilled over into emerging markets in other regions.

The final three regressions reported in Table 2 represent experiments with more restricted versions of the equations described above. In the third and fourth columns, the separate Rating*Year-Dummy variables are replaced by a single interaction term, Rating*Mexico, the "Mexico" dummy variable is 1 if a bond or loan is issued in 1995 or later, and 0 otherwise. The coefficient on this variable is highly significant, and the adjusted R^2 remains unchanged.

Finally, in the fifth column, the separate year dummies are replaced by a "Time Trend" term and the Mexico dummy described above. "Time Trend" takes on the value 1991 if the instrument was issued in 1991, 1992 if the instrument was issued in 1992, and so on. As expected, there is a significant negative coefficient on the time trend, indicating a secular decline in spreads in the 1990s, and also a significant negative coefficient on the Mexico dummy, indicating the acceleration in declines in spreads for the best-rated instruments in the wake of the Mexican financial crisis. The interaction term, Rating*Mexico, remains highly significant, while the adjusted R^2 is again unchanged. The results of the fifth regression presented in Table 2 suggest that, to a first approximation, the evolution over the 1990s of emerging market credit spreads can be compactly described by a time trend and a level effect associated with the Mexican financial crisis whose magnitude depends on the credit rating of the instrument. The question of whether or not this pattern can be traced, in part, to movements in industrial country interest rates is addressed in Section 3 below.

2.2 *A simulated measure of emerging market spreads*

Chart 5 presents simulations of the equation presented in the second regression column of Table 2 for the evolution of spreads (shown in basis points) on dollar-denominated 10-year bonds of different credit ratings. The simulations themselves are straightforward. To calculate the spread of a BB dollar-denominated 10-year bond in 1994, for example, we specify an equation with all the explanatory variables indicated in the left-hand column of Table 2, multiplied by the coefficients shown in the second regression column (the one labelled "Bonds").

We then set the Rating variable to the appropriate numerical value for a BB instrument (12), set the Term variable to 10, set the currency dummy variables to 0, set the year dummies for all years except 1994 to 0, and set the 1994-Dummy variable to 1. We then multiply all explanatory variables by their coefficients to get the log of the predicted spread, and then take the exponent to calculate the spread itself.

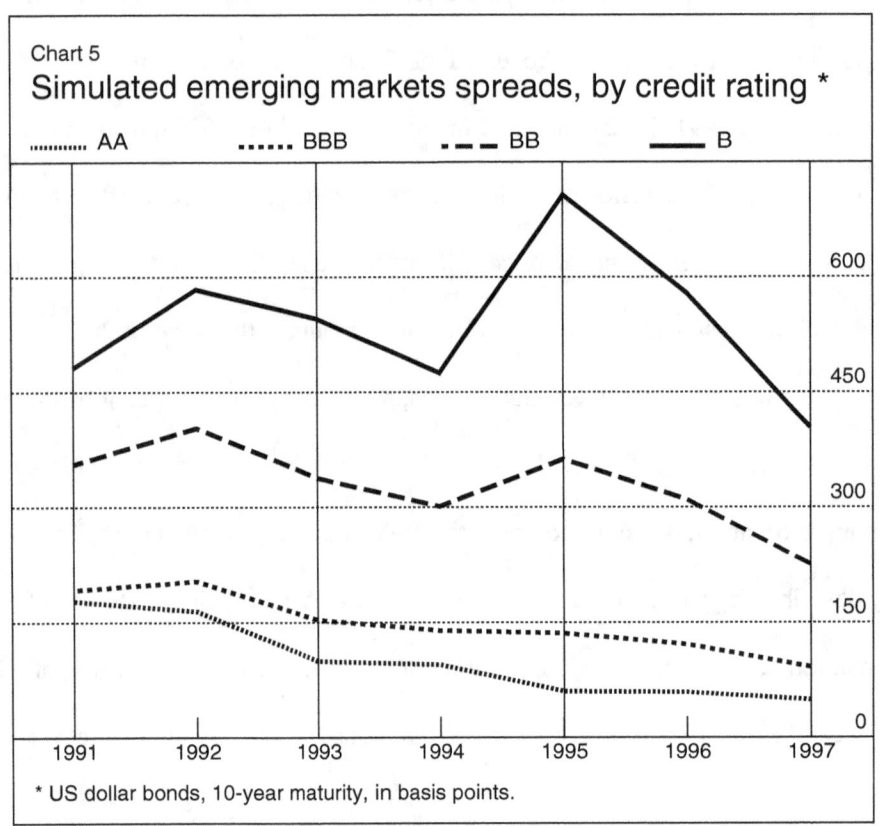

Chart 5 clarifies the various trends experienced by emerging market spreads in the 1990s, prior to the Asian crisis. First, for all types of borrowers, and holding all characteristics of debt instruments and borrowers constant, there has been a long-term decline in spreads, which by mid-1997 were at their lowest points in the decade. Second, for emerging market borrowers with investment grade ratings, BBB and better, this trend was not interrupted by the Mexican financial crisis; in fact, the most highly rated borrowers appear to have benefited from the "flight to quality" through an acceleration in the decline in their spreads, although the BBB-rated borrowers appear to have not been affected one way or the other. Finally, spreads on speculative grade borrowers, BB and below, surged in 1995. Much of their subsequent decline appears to be mainly a return to their former trend path, suggesting that market commentators may have read too much into the decline in emerging market spreads in the previous two years.

The movements in spreads indicated in Chart 5 are clearly more plausible and coherent than the weighted-average spreads on bonds and loans shown in Chart 1. This indicates the importance of controlling for credit quality and maturity when examining market spreads. Additionally, it is clear that the pattern of movement of Brady bond spreads shown in Chart 1 is similar to that of B-rated bonds shown in Chart 5, but very different from the patterns exhibited by the BBB- and AA-rated bonds shown in that chart. These comparisons further underscore the fact that spreads on Brady bonds, while perhaps consistent with those on other relatively poorly rated instruments, may not be reflective of the financing costs of emerging market borrowers more generally.

2.3 *A comparison of credit spreads in different regions*

In this section we address two related questions. First, do international investors discriminate among different regions of the developing world, that is, for given ratings and maturities, are borrowers in certain regions required to pay higher spreads than borrowers in other regions? Second, might the surge in spreads for speculative grade borrowers in 1995, shown in Chart 5, have been limited to Latin American borrowers alone, with spreads for speculative grade borrowers in other regions showing a more muted response to the Mexican financial crisis?

The regression reported in the first column of Table 4 addresses the first question listed above. Dummy variables are included that take on the value of 1 if an issue is from a particular region and 0 if not. No dummy for Asian countries is included, so the value of the coefficient on another regional dummy represents the difference between the spread on an issue from that region and the spread on an Asian issue with the same rating, term, currency denomination, and year of issue. The results indicate that borrowers from three regions of the developing world paid significantly higher spreads than Asian borrowers, at least prior to the Asian financial crisis. Spreads on Latin American issues with the same characteristics as Asian issues are 39% higher,[21] spreads on issues from offshore centres (such as the Bahamas or Cayman islands) are 21% higher, and spreads on eastern European issues are 19% higher.

It is not clear why spreads on issues from certain regions are systematically higher than those on issues from other regions. One possibility is that investors systematically differ in their assessments of creditworthiness from the commercial ratings agencies. Another possibility is that investors and credit ratings agencies share the same estimates of expected default, but that investors also charge a premium for greater uncertainty about current and prospective creditworthiness. Insofar as, at least until recently, Latin American and eastern European economies have exhibited greater volatility than Asian economies, the higher spreads charged to their borrowers may reflect a premium for higher uncertainty.[22]

To begin to explore the relationship between investor discrimination among regions and the Mexican financial crisis, the second column of Table 4 presents a regression in which a dummy variable has been entered for Latin American issues alone. As expected, this coefficient is positive and highly significant, indicating that Latin American borrowers pay significantly more than borrowers in the other regions, taken together.

---

[21] By contrast, Min (1998) fails to identify significant regional effects on spreads.

[22] A third possibility, suggested by Eichengreen and Mody (1998a), who also find higher spreads for Latin American bonds, is that Latin America tended to issue more bonds than other regions, thereby raising the supply of its bonds and lowering their price (thereby raising spreads). However, this explanation does not appear to explain the results of our research, insofar as we include both bond and loan spreads in our sample, and Asian countries, while tending to issue less bonds than Latin America, also tended to take out more loans.

Table 4

Emerging market spreads over industrial country benchmarks: Regional effects*

Dependent variable: log (spread)

	All Regions	Latin America 1	Latin America 2
Africa – Dummy	–0.10		
	(–0.50)		
Middle East – Dummy	0.06		
	(0.58)		
Eastern Europe – Dummy	0.18		
	(2.98)		
Offshore Centres – Dummy	0.19		
	(2.07)		
Latin America – Dummy	0.33	0.26	
	(7.66)	(6.59)	
Latin America – pre-1995 – Dummy			0.24
			(3.71)
Latin America – post-1994 – Dummy			0.27
			(5.52)
1991 – Dummy	2.22	3.09	3.00
	(0.82)	(1.14)	(1.09)
1992 – Dummy	0.96	0.89	0.88
	(3.70)	(3.43)	(3.29)
1993 – Dummy	0.94	0.93	0.92
	(4.50)	(4.45)	(4.27)
1994 – Dummy	0.89	0.85	0.84
	(4.17)	(3.97)	(3.82)
1995 – Dummy	0.19	0.14	0.14
	(0.92)	(0.69)	(0.70)
1996 – Dummy	0.15	0.12	0.12
	(0.78)	(0.65)	(0.65)
Rating * 1991 – Dummy	–0.15	–0.22	–0.21
	(–0.67)	(–0.98)	(–0.92)
Rating * 1992 – Dummy	–0.04	–0.04	–0.04
	(–1.70)	(–1.50)	(–1.33)
Rating * 1993 – Dummy	–0.04	–0.04	–0.04
	(–2.20)	(–2.14)	(–1.87)
Rating * 1994 – Dummy	–0.05	–0.04	–0.04
	(–2.24)	(–2.05)	(–1.81)
Rating * 1995 – Dummy	0.02	0.03	0.03
	(1.22)	(1.45)	(1.45)
Rating * 1996 – Dummy	0.02	0.02	0.02
	(0.86)	(0.99)	(0.98)
Adj. R – Square	0.82	0.82	0.82
No. of observations	662	662	662

* Coefficients on intercept, bond dummy, ratings, term, and currency denomination not shown; they are similar to those shown in Table 2.

Finally, in the third regression reported in Table 4, the Latin America dummy is split into two components: one dummy if the issue is Latin American and it was issued before 1995, the other dummy for if the issue is Latin American and it was issued in 1995 or after. The purpose of this regression is to test the hypothesis that before the Mexican financial crisis, Latin American borrowers were treated the same as those from other regions, but that afterwards, they were charged a special risk premium. The results convincingly refute this hypothesis. First, the coefficients on the two Latin American dummies are approximately equal, suggesting that Latin American borrowers were charged the same premium over borrowers from other regions both before and after the Mexican financial crisis. Second, the pattern of coefficients on the Year and Rating*Year dummies remain unchanged, suggesting that for other regions besides Latin America, gaps between spreads on speculative grade and investment grade instruments widened after 1994. In sum, the apparent effects of the Mexican financial crisis documented in our regressions and in Chart 3 were not limited to Latin American borrowers alone.

3. The role of industrial country interest rates

In this section, we consider the extent to which variations in industrial country interest rates can help to explain the pattern of movement of emerging market spreads shown in Chart 5. In particular, we assess the view that declines in industrial country interest rates were responsible for declines in emerging market spreads.

3.1 *Linkages between industrial country interest rates and emerging market spreads*

In principle, there are a number of reasons why changes in industrial country interest rates could (positively) affect emerging market credit spreads. First, there is what might be termed the "mathematical" effect that the yield on a safe instrument exerts on the spread over that safe yield of a risky instrument. Consider a highly simplified example involving two one-period interest rates: r, the rate on a safe instrument such as a treasury bill, and i, the rate on a risky instrument that is repaid with probability $p<1$. In equilibrium,

$$(1 + r) = p(1 + i) + (1 - p)0$$

This implies the following formula for the spread:

$$i - r = (1 + r)(1 - p)/p$$

Clearly, as long as $p<1$, increases in the safe interest rate r lead to increases in the spread, i-r. Intuitively, increases in the safe interest rate lead to an increase in the amount that has to be repaid by a risky borrower; because the risky borrower is not certain to repay the full amount of that rise, however, the yield on the risky instrument must rise by even more than that on the safe instrument to compensate. Hence, changes in industrial country benchmark yields are likely to lead to changes in emerging market spreads over those yields for "mathematical" reasons alone.

A second reason why changes in industrial country interest rates may affect emerging market spreads is that these changes may affect borrower creditworthiness. An increase in industrial country interest rates increases the debt service burden borne by borrower countries, thereby reducing their ability to repay their debts and hence lowering their creditworthiness. This, in turn, can lead to increases in spreads paid by borrower countries.

Finally, there is the effect of industrial country interest rates on "appetite for risk". As discussed in the introduction to this paper, a view commonly expressed in the financial press was that the decline of emerging market spreads could be attributed to a generalised decline in industrial country interest rates. According to this view, international investors attempt to enhance portfolio returns in a low interest rate environment by increasing their risk exposure. On this reasoning, spreads on risky assets in general, and emerging market debt instruments in particular, are positively related to levels of short-term interest rates in the industrial countries. Therefore, declines in industrial country interest rates can lead to declines in spreads on emerging market instruments.

It should be noted that we have not seen any research establishing a theoretical justification for the "appetite for risk" argument. That is, it is not obvious that the positive relationship between industrial country interest rates and spreads posited by that argument is consistent with rational, maximizing behaviour in financial markets. However, given the prominence of the "appetite for risk" argument in much financial market commentary, we still believe it to be worthwhile to explore the empirical support for this argument.

3.2 Analysis of new-issue bond spreads

As a test of the hypothesis that the levels of industrial country interest rates influence emerging market spreads, we added various measures of industrial country interest rates to regression equations for new-issue bond spreads. These regressions included as control variables the measures of creditworthiness, maturity, currency denomination, and region of issue described in Section 2.

The results of these regressions are presented in Tables 5a, 5b, and 5c; in each of these tables, the coefficients on the control variables are not shown, but are essentially similar to those presented in Tables 2 and 4.

Turning to Table 5a, the first column indicates the results of an equation in which the benchmark yield alone, that is, the yield on the industrial country government bond with the same maturity and currency as the emerging market bond, on approximately the same day as the emerging market bond was issued, is added as an explanatory variable. The second column indicates the results when the yield on a bond issued by the same government as that which issued the benchmark bond, but of only one year's maturity, is used. This 1-year benchmark yield, as it is labeled in Table 5a, is intended to reflect the stance of industrial country monetary policy and hence industrial country liquidity. Therefore, it is likely to better identify "appetite for risk" effects on emerging market spreads than a longer term interest rate, which is affected by industrial country inflation expectations and hence may not capture liquidity effects as precisely.

Finally, the third column of Table 5a includes both the benchmark yield and the 1-year benchmark yield. In principle, with "mathematical" effects being captured by the coefficient on the benchmark yield and with the effects of interest rates on borrower creditworthiness being held

Table 5a

Coefficients on industrial country interest rates*

Dependent variable: log (spread)

	(1)	(2)	(3)	(4)	(5)	(6)
Benchmark yield	−0.0002 (−0.80)		0.0004 (0.89)	0.0000 (0.05)		−0.0003 (−0.70)
1-year benchmark yield		−0.0003 (−1.32)	−0.0004 (−1.40)		0.0003 (1.62)	0.0005 (1.55)
Mexico Dummy				−0.33 (−2.15)	−0.37 (−2.36)	−0.38 (−2.39)
Rating & Mexico Dummy				0.05 (4.40)	0.06 (4.72)	0.06 (4.68)
Time trend				−0.14 (−5.52)	−0.15 (−5.56)	−0.15 (−5.51)
Adj. R-Square	0.79	0.78	0.78	0.82	0.82	0.82
No. of observations	302	283	281	302	283	281

* Coefficients on intercept, ratings, term, currency denomination, and region are not shown (t-statistics in parentheses).

constant by the inclusion of credit ratings as an explanatory variable,[23] the coefficient on the 1-year benchmark yield in this equation should largely reflect "appetite for risk" effects. In fact, however, the coefficients on both the benchmark yield and the 1-year benchmark yield are statistically insignificant in all of the equations in columns 1 to 3, and in most cases are of the wrong sign as well. These results suggest, on the face of it, that variations in industrial country interest rates have made no contribution to the evolution of emerging market bond spreads.

---

[23] In fact, it is well known that credit ratings agencies are slow to adjust ratings in responses to changes in a borrower's situation. Therefore, it is an open question as to how well the inclusion of the credit rating variable controls for this particular channel through which industrial country interest rates affect emerging market spreads.

Table 5b
Coefficients on industrial country interest rates*
Dependent variable: log (spread)

	(1)	(2)	(3)	(4)	(5)	(6)
Benchmark yield	−0.0002 (−0.80)		−0.0008 (−2.82)	0.0000 (.05)		−0.0004 (−1.28)
1-year G-3 yield		0.0004 (1.24)	0.0011 (2.62)		0.0001 (.37)	0.0005 (1.10)
Mexico Dummy				−0.33 (−2.15)	−0.36 (−2.34)	−0.37 (−2.37)
Rating & Mexico Dummy				0.05 (4.40)	0.06 (4.59)	0.06 (4.57)
Time trend				−0.14 (−5.52)	−0.13 (−5.06)	−0.12 (−4.58)
Adj. R-Square	0.79	0.80	0.80	0.82	0.82	0.83
No. of observations	302	294	292	302	294	292

* Coefficients on intercept, ratings, term, currency denomination, and region are not shown (t-statistics in parentheses).

Columns 4 to 6 of Table 5a present the results of equations that are similar to those in columns 1 to 3, but with the addition of a time trend and dummies for the Mexican financial crisis, as in the fifth column of Table 2. With these variables included to account for longer-term trends in the spread, as well as the effects of the Mexico crisis, it might be possible to better identify an independent effect of industrial country interest rates. As may be seen, however, while the coefficient on the 1-year benchmark yield now switches to the expected sign, it remains insignificantly different from zero, as does the coefficient on the benchmark yield. Conversely, the values and significance levels of the coefficients on the time trend and Mexico dummies are largely unchanged from their values in the fifth column of Table 2, when no industrial country interest rates were included.

To test for the robustness of these results to different industrial country interest rates, Table 5b presents regression results in which the benchmark yield is kept the same as in Table 5a (columns 1 and 4 are the same as in Table 5a, and are repeated merely for ease of comparison), but the 1-year benchmark yield, the yield on a 1-year industrial country government bond of the same currency denomination as the emerging market bond, is replaced by a GDP-weighted average of one-year yields in the United States, Germany and Japan (the G-3 countries).[24] This specification was chosen to consider the possibility that the behaviour of industrial country investors might be influenced not only by interest rates in their own country, but in other major industrial countries as well. As indicated in Table 5b, however, the coefficient on the 1-year G-3 yield is statistically significant and of the expected sign only in the equation shown in column 3. Inclusion of the time trend and the Mexico dummies effectively wipes this coefficient out, suggesting that the variable was merely proxying for other factors. Moreover, in the column 3 equation, the coefficient on the benchmark yield is also statistically significant, but of the *wrong* sign.

Table 5c
Coefficients on industrial country interest rates*
Dependent variable: log (spread)

	(1)	(2)	(3)	(4)	(5)	(6)
Benchmark yield	−0.0002 (−0.80)		−0.0003 (−1.22)	0.0000 (0.05)		0.0000 (0.2683)
1-year Japan yield		0.0588 (3.76)	0.0595 (3.75)		−0.0139 (−0.44)	−0.0175 (−0.51)
Mexico Dummy				−0.33 (−2.15)	−0.33 (−2.17)	−0.34 (−2.17)
Rating & Mexico Dummy				0.05 (4.40)	0.05 (4.30)	0.05 (4.25)
Time trend				−0.14 (−5.52)	−0.14 (−4.76)	−0.15 (−4.59)
Adj. R-Square	0.79	0.80	0.80	0.82	0.82	0.82
No. of observations	302	301	299	302	301	299

* Coefficients on intercept, ratings, term, currency denomination, and region are not shown (t-statistics in parentheses).

---

[24] A weight of 0.55 was applied to the US rate, a weight of 0.30 to the Japanese rate and a weight of 0.15 was given to the German rate.

Finally, in Table 5c, the 1-year G-3 yield is replaced by the 1-year yield on Japanese government bonds alone. This specification was adopted to take into account assertions by some market observers that increases in Japanese liquidity had been driving down credit spreads on many countries' bonds, regardless of their currency denomination. In the regressions that exclude the time trend and Mexico dummies, the coefficient on the 1-year Japanese rate is positive and highly significant. However, as in the case of the G-3 rate, inclusion of the time trend and Mexico dummies causes this coefficient to be insignificantly different from zero and causes its sign to become negative as well. As in the case of the G-3 rate, therefore, it is likely that the Japanese rate was proxying for other factors, most likely a time trend, and that once a time trend was included, variations in the Japanese rate yielded no additional explanatory power.

In sum, our analysis of new-issue bond spreads provides little support for the view that industrial country interest rates have exerted a significant influence over emerging market bond spreads.

3.3 Analysis of Brady bond spreads

Because the results described above were at such variance with market commentary concerning the relationship between industrial country interest rates and emerging market spreads, we thought it would be useful to assess whether spreads on Brady bonds might be more closely linked with industrial country rates. This comparison is particularly apt, as market commentary probably has been informed more by Brady bond spreads than by new issue spreads.

Chart 6a compares the evolution of the J P Morgan monthly weighted average of stripped spreads on Brady bonds to three different measures of industrial country short rates: the three-month US Treasury bill rate, a weighted average of G-3 three-month interest rates, and the Japanese three-month rate.[25] On the face of it, the Brady bond spreads and industrial country

---

[25] For Germany, the 3-month interbank loan rate is used. For Japan, a 3-month certificate of deposit rate is used. The weights in the G-3 average are the same as in the G-3 1-year yield used to analyse new-issue spreads: United States (0.55), Japan (0.30), and Germany (0.15).

interest rates (or, at least, the US and G-3 rates) share some similar broad swings: declines from 1991 to 1993, increases to 1994, and declines thereafter.

If the "appetite for risk" hypothesis is correct, however, Brady bonds and industrial country interest rates should share more than merely the broadest swings, as these co-movements might merely reflect correlations of both variables with other factors that are moving over time. Chart 6b compares month-to-month differences in Brady bond spreads with differences in industrial country interest rates. Here, correlations between the two variables are less obvious.

In order to evaluate the relationship between Brady bond spreads and industrial country interest rates more formally, Tables 6a to 6d present the results of estimating econometric equations for Brady spreads. Table 6a evaluates the relationship between Brady bond spreads and the three-month US Treasury bill rate. The first column examines the relationship, over the entire sample period, between the levels of the two variables, including a trend term and a dummy variable for the first three months of 1995 as control variables. While the coefficient on the treasury bill rate is positive and statistically significant, the equation is subject to extreme autocorrelation. Moreover, augmented Dickey-Fuller tests (not shown) indicated that all of the variables examined, Brady bond spreads and all industrial country interest rates, are non-stationary in their levels, although they are stationary in their differences.

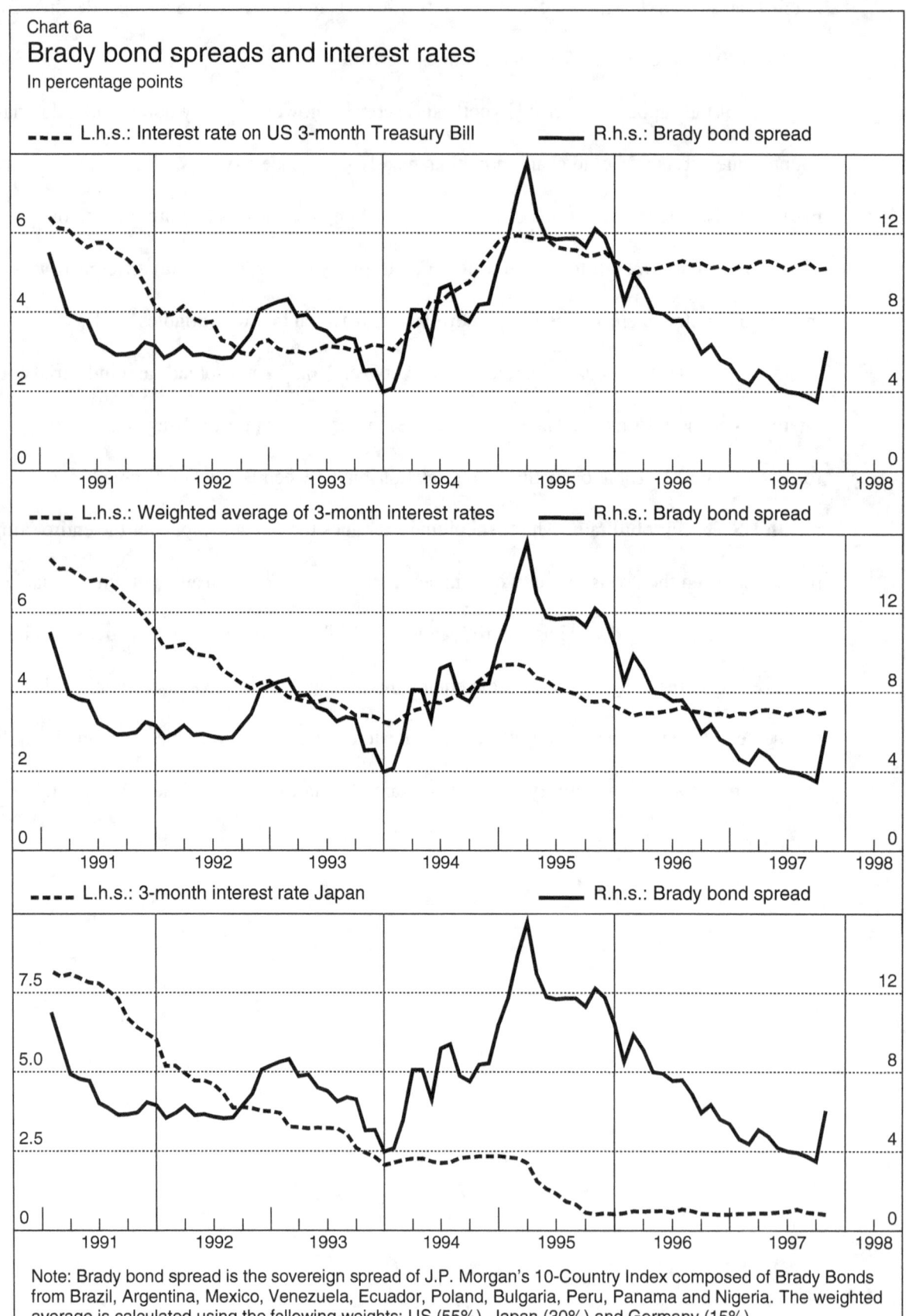

Chart 6a
Brady bond spreads and interest rates
In percentage points

Note: Brady bond spread is the sovereign spread of J.P. Morgan's 10-Country Index composed of Brady Bonds from Brazil, Argentina, Mexico, Venezuela, Ecuador, Poland, Bulgaria, Peru, Panama and Nigeria. The weighted average is calculated using the following weights: US (55%), Japan (30%) and Germany (15%).

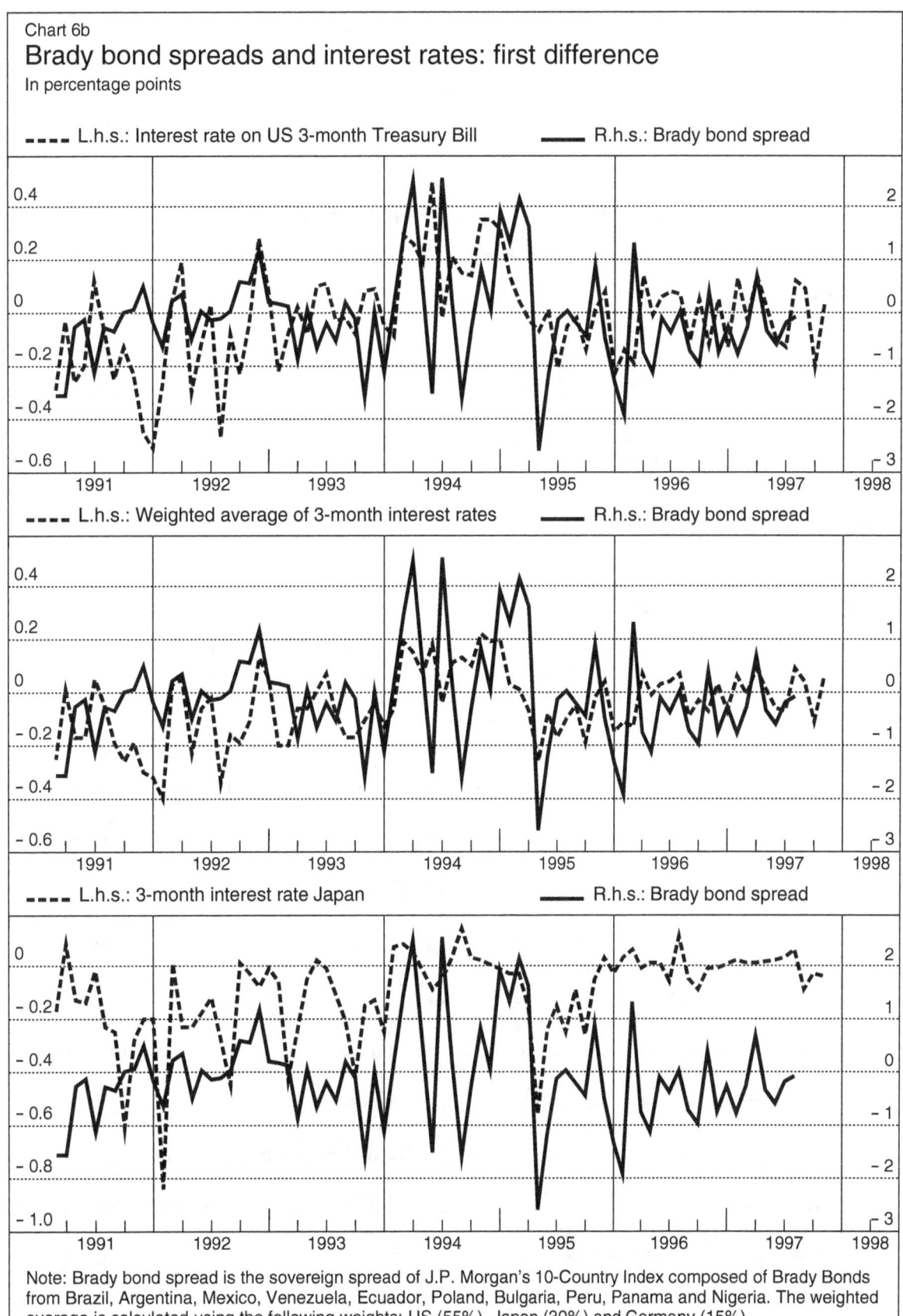

Table 6a

Effect of industrial country interest rates on brady bond spreads

Dependent variable: Spread or Δ Spread

(monthly data)

	(1) 1991.1-1997.6 Levels	(2) 1991.1-1997.6 Differences	(3) 1991.1-1994.12 Levels	(4) 1991.1-1994.12 Differences	(5) 1995.1-1997.6 Levels	(6) 1995.1-1997.6 Differences
Intercept	375.68 (3.53)	14.28 (0.65)	319.64 (3.11)	−15.54 (−0.43)	2814.12 (3.94)	−206.96 (−1.54)
3-month US Treasury rate*	82.76 (3.51)	125.00 (2.22)	71.70 (3.69)	89.98 (1.17)	54.29 (0.52)	−65.91 (−0.46)
1995-Q1 Dummy	516.78 (4.14)	169.59 (3.26)			−6.54 (−0.09)	264.82 (3.96)
Time trend	−0.18 (−0.16)	−0.64 (−1.36)	3.58 (2.35)	0.76 (0.59)	−35.11 (−11.29)	2.50 (1.22)
Adj. R-Square	0.32	0.17	0.21	0.05	0.93	0.38
D.W.	0.27	1.92	0.47	1.78	1.39	2.12
No. of observations	78	76	48	46	30	30

* In equations (2), (4), and (6), this variable is lagged by one month (t-statistics in parentheses).

Therefore, it is more useful to examine the second column, which presents the regression results for differenced Brady bond spreads and (one-period lagged)[26] treasury bill rates. Here, too, the coefficient on the treasury bill rate is positive and significant, and there is no evidence of serial correlation in the error term. This result appears to confirm the predicted linkage between industrial country interest rates and emerging market spreads. However, this linkage breaks down when the equations using differenced data are estimated for the sub-periods before and after the Mexican devaluation at the end of 1994. As evidenced by the results shown in columns 4 and 6, in neither of the sub-periods is the coefficient on the differenced treasury bill rates positive and significant. This casts considerable doubt on the robustness of the relationship between Brady bond spreads and US interest rates.

---

[26] Some initial experimentation suggested that for 3-month treasury bill rates, the lagged rate was better correlated with Brady bond spreads than the contemporaneous rate.

Table 6b
Effect of industrial country interest rates on brady bond spreads
Dependent variable: Spread or Δ Spread
(monthly data)

	(1) 1991.1-1997.6 Levels	(2) 1991.1-1997.6 Differences	(3) 1991.1-1994.12 Levels	(4) 1991.1-1994.12 Differences	(5) 1995.1-1997.6 Levels	(6) 1995.1-1997.6 Differences
Intercept	671.00	2.38	366.00	−36.00	3615.05	−198.20
	(1.67)	(0.11)	(−1.29)	(−1.21)	(10.29)	(−1.44)
30-year US Treasury yield*	4.99	63.11	127.83	52.32	−70.94	−14.31
	(0.10)	(1.21)	(3.70)	(0.72)	(−1.36)	(−0.19)
1995-Q1 Dummy	615.43	199.67			83.75	248.68
	(4.55)	(3.76)			(1.02)	(4.34)
Time trend	0.98	−0.40	4.80	1.50	−35.67	2.39
	(0.66)	(−0.86)	(2.86)	(1.44)	(−16.56)	(1.14)
Adj. R-Square	0.21	0.13	0.21	0.03	0.93	0.38
D.W.	0.27	1.92	0.47	1.86	1.32	2.09
No. of observations	78	76	48	46	30	30

* In equations (2), (4), and (6), this variable is lagged by one month (t-statistics in parentheses).

Table 6c
Effect of industrial country interest rates on brady bond spreads
Dependent variable: Spread or Δ Spread
(monthly data)

	(1) 1991.1-1997.6 Levels	(2) 1991.1-1997.6 Differences	(3) 1991.1-1994.12 Levels	(4) 1991.1-1994.12 Differences	(5) 1995.1-1997.6 Levels	(6) 1995.1-1997.6 Differences
Intercept	387.21	15.37	−51.60	−46.45	3812.03	−82.43
	(1.86)	(0.66)	(−0.27)	(−1.23)	(5.52)	(−0.54)
3-month G-3 interest rate	55.78	175.42	110.11	23.78	−1.01	252.38
	(1.60)	(2.20)	(3.81)	(0.22)	(−0.01)	(1.27)
1995-Q1 Dummy	576.03	187.12			10.37	218.21
	(4.38)	(3.60)			(0.12)	(3.60)
Time trend	2.99	−0.57	9.67	1.86	−36.29	0.78
	(1.74)	(−1.18)	(3.74)	(1.49)	(−10.21)	(0.35)
Adj. R-Square	0.24	0.17	0.22	0.05	0.93	0.41
D.W.	0.26	1.97	0.48	1.76	1.35	2.27
No. of observations	78	77	48	47	30	30

(t-statistics in parentheses)

Table 6d
Effect of industrial country interest rates on brady bond spreads
Dependent variable: Spread or Δ Spread
(monthly data)

	(1) 1991.1-1997.6 Levels	(2) 1991.1-1997.6 Differences	(3) 1991.1-1994.12 Levels	(4) 1991.1-1994.12 Differences	(5) 1995.1-1997.6 Levels	(6) 1995.1-1997.6 Differences
Intercept	1020.23	15.85	−138.08	−49.89	3403.55	35.91
	(4.71)	(0.63)	(−0.60)	(−1.45)	(15.69)	(0.23)
3-month Japan interest rate	−45.94	113.30	106.09	8.54	−111.13	299.41
	(−1.47)	(1.76)	(3.55)	(0.11)	(−1.36)	(2.24)
1995-Q1 Dummy	634.15	191.16			147.67	206.10
	(4.89)	(3.64)			(1.25)	(3.69)
Time trend	−3.57	−0.53	15.98	1.99	−38.60	−0.95
	(−1.11)	(−1.07)	(3.66)	(1.87)	(−14.16)	(−0.41)
Adj. R-Square	0.24	0.15	0.20	0.05	0.93	0.48
D.W.	0.28	1.83	0.48	1.75	1.30	1.98
No. of observations	78	77	48	47	30	30

(t-statistics in parentheses)

Table 6b presents similar regressions that use the 30-year treasury bond yield as an explanatory variable instead of the 3-month treasury bill rate. While the 30-year bond yield is likely to be a less precise measure of monetary stance and liquidity–it is affected by expectations of future US inflation that, in principle, should not have a bearing on Brady bond spreads–some observers have suggested that it is a better predictor of emerging market spreads than the 3-month rate. However, the results presented in Table 6b indicate that the 30-year treasury bond yield is even more poorly correlated with Brady bond spreads than the 3-month rate.

Finally, Tables 6c and 6d indicate the estimation results based on the G-3 weighted-average and Japanese 3-month rates. Again, they show little indication of a strong and robust linkage between those rates and Brady bond spreads.

3.4 A comparison with other studies

Our failure to identify a strong positive linkage between industrial country interest rates and emerging market spreads is consistent with the results of other recent studies that, while not always focused on the role of industrial country interest rates *per se*, include them as explanatory variables in their models. Cline and Barnes (1997) estimate a regression to explain Eurobond spreads for twelve emerging market countries and six industrial countries during 1992–96. The explanatory variables include standard country creditworthiness indicators (debt/exports, reserves/imports, etc.), as well as the US 10-year Treasury bond interest rate. The coefficient on the treasury bond rate is estimated to be positive but highly insignificant (t-statistic of 0.23).

Eichengreen and Mody (1998a) analyse a dataset of new bond issue spreads drawn from the Capital DATA Bondware database, much as in our study, and estimate a model to explain simultaneously both the probability of emerging market bond issuance and the spread. They find that declines in 10-year US Treasury bond rates lead to increases in the issuance of bonds by emerging market countries–consistent with the findings of Calvo, Leiderman, and Reinhart (1993) for the effects of US interest rates on capital flows–but also to *increases*, not decreases, in the spreads on these bonds. They interpret their results as suggesting that declines in US interest rates cause increases in the supply of emerging market bonds that lower their price and hence raise their spread. While declines in US interest rates may also raise the demand for emerging market bonds, which might tend, all else equal, to lower spreads, this effect is dominated by the effect of increased bond issuance. Further investigation presented in Eichengreen and Mody (1998b), in which the supply and demand for emerging market bonds are estimated simultaneously, is generally supportive of this hypothesis.

Min (1998) also analyses new bond issue spreads drawn from Capital DATA Bondware, measuring their sensitivity to a broad array of standard creditworthiness indicators, regional dummies, period dummies, and maturity measures. Like Cline and Barnes (1997) (but unlike Eichengreen and Mody, 1998a), he finds a measure of industrial country interest rates, the 3-month US Treasury bill rate, to have a positive but insignificant impact on emerging market bond spreads.

Hence, all three recent studies lend support to the evidence reported in our own study that the decline in industrial country interest rates in recent years does not explain the decline in emerging market spreads. These results find further support in research applied to US corporate spreads. In principle, if the "appetite for risk" argument is correct, declines in industrial country interest rates might be expected to lead to declines not only in spreads on emerging market debt instruments, but also in spreads on industrial country corporate bonds. It is beyond the scope of this paper to analyse directly the empirical relationship between interest rates and corporate spreads in industrial countries. However, in an examination of this issue for corporations in the United States, Duffee (1996) estimated a negative relationship between the level of US Treasury bond yields and the spread on US corporate bonds, that is, declines in bond yield tended to raise, not lower, corporate spreads. This result mirrors that found by Eichengreen and Mody (1998a) for emerging market bonds.

3.5 A qualification

In sum, both direct evidence on emerging market bond spreads, both for new issues and in the secondary market, and indirect evidence from the US corporate bond markets cast doubt upon the hypothesis that reductions in emerging market spreads are attributable to the decline in industrial country interest rates. However, owing to the fact that the phenomenon we are analysing is relatively short-lived (our data start only in 1991, about when emerging market bonds began to be issued in earnest), an important qualification is in order. We have documented the fact that relatively high frequency movements in industrial country interest rates cannot explain the movements in emerging market bond spreads. However, it is possible that the relationship between industrial country interest rates and emerging market spreads is of a much longer-term nature, so that shorter-term movements in the two factors are poorly correlated.

For example, declines in industrial country interest rates may lead to a demand for riskier assets that, in turn, leads to institutional changes such as the expansion of credit ratings activities, the development of investing and monitoring capacity in new regions, and even a re-direction of savings from bank deposits to mutual funds and other vehicles more likely to be invested abroad. It is those institutional changes that facilitate the rise in investment flows that leads ultimately to lower spreads. In this scenario, temporary increases in industrial country interest rates may not lead immediately to a contraction in the infrastructure required for international investment, and hence may not lead immediately to a full reversal of previous declines in emerging market spreads. In this sense, declines in industrial country interest rates may actually be a cause of globalisation, rather than an alternative explanation for declining emerging market spreads.

At this point in time, however, the scenario described above is speculative and will require more years of data to test. Moreover, the results shown in Tables 5a to 5c have an important implication for policy-makers in the near term. They imply that, regardless of the long-term relationship between industrial country interest rates and emerging market spreads, a future upturn in interest rates may lead to a smaller upturn in emerging market spreads than some observers are anticipating.

4. Conclusion

Based on the research described in this paper, we can draw the following conclusions. First, movements in spreads on Brady bonds, which remain the most common index of emerging market spreads, are not representative of trends in all emerging market credit spreads. Not only are Brady bond spreads considerably higher than average emerging market spreads, in large part reflecting the relatively low credit rating of their issuers, but their behaviour during the Mexican financial crisis exhibited considerably higher volatility than did spreads on the many investment grade emerging market credits issued at the time.

Second, spreads on emerging market instruments have strong and well-defined relationships to credit rating, maturity, and currency denomination. We determined that while spreads on bonds were systematically higher than spreads on banks loans, the responses of spreads on the two types of instruments to changes in other determinants, ratings, maturity, etc., were very similar. We also determined that, holding all other factors constant, investors systematically have charged borrowers in Latin America and eastern Europe higher spreads than borrowers in Asia and the Middle East.

Third, in order to analyse underlying movements in emerging market credit spreads over time, changes in credit rating, maturity, and the other determinants of spreads must be controlled for. This was accomplished by simulating our equation for credit spreads over the course of the 1990s, allowing for changes only in our time variables. Based on these simulations, we determined that spreads on emerging market debt instruments declined in the years leading up to the Asian financial crisis by more than can be explained by improvements in risk factors–credit ratings and maturity–alone.

Moreover, credit issues with different ratings showed very different patterns of movements during the decade. Spreads on investment grade instruments declined throughout the 1990s, until the advent of the Asian crisis, with that decline accelerating in 1995, probably due to a "flight to quality" during the Mexican financial crisis. Conversely, spreads on speculative grade instruments, after declining prior to 1995, surged upward in 1995 before slowly returning to their trend paths by early 1997. In this regard, spreads on speculative grade instruments appear to have been relatively well correlated with Brady bond spreads, while there was much less correlation between the spreads on investment grade instruments and Brady bonds.

Finally, we attempted to determine the extent to which the decline in emerging market spreads during the 1990s, up until the advent of the Asian financial crisis, could be attributed to declines in industrial country interest rates, as suggested by many market observers. We found that we could identify no robust, statistically significant relationship between various measures of industrial country interest rates and emerging market new-issue bond spreads. Conversely, regardless of equation specification, these spreads were shown to have been influenced by a statistically significant declining trend over the course of the 1990s, prior to the Asian crisis, as well as by statistically significant effects of the Mexican financial crisis. To the extent that the declining trend in spreads can be associated with an on-going process of financial globalisation, and this is merely a speculation at this point, this suggests that the main causes of declines in emerging market spreads were a combination of globalisation and, more recently, the dissipation of the Mexican financial crisis.

Our failure to find a strong, robust, positive linkage between industrial country interest rates and spreads on new issues of emerging market bonds was mirrored by similar findings for Brady bond spreads. Additionally, other recent studies of spreads, both on emerging market instruments and on US corporate bonds, also find evidence contradicting the view that declines in industrial country interest rates were responsible for declines in emerging market spreads. Nevertheless, our results are subject to several qualifications.

First, as noted earlier in this paper, declines in industrial country interest rates, to the extent that they lead to greater capital flows to emerging market countries, may cause increases in exposure to emerging market borrowers that cause spreads to rise, offsetting an "appetite for risk" effect that otherwise would lead to lower spreads. (See Eichengreen and Mody, 1998a and 1998b.) Therefore, even if declines in industrial country interest rates cannot explain the decline in emerging market spreads through mid-1977, industrial country interest rates may still importantly affect the overall terms of access of emerging market countries to international capital markets.

Secondly, as also noted above, the linkage between industrial country interest rates and emerging market spreads may operate over a much longer horizon and on a lower-frequency basis than we have been able to explore to date. This hypothesis will be difficult to test directly until more years of data are available. However, it may be useful to examine certain corollaries of this hypothesis, including the effect of industrial country interest rates on household portfolio decisions, on the allocation of savings between banks, mutual funds, and other vehicles, and on the activities of credit rating firms and other agencies that help to support the flow of portfolio capital to emerging markets.

References

Ammer, John (1997): "Sovereign Credit Ratings and International Debt Markets". *Mimeo*, Federal Reserve Board.

Andrews, David and Shogo Ishii (1995): "The Mexican Financial Crisis: A Test of the Resilience of the Markets for Developing Country Securities". *IMF Working Paper* WP/95/132.

Calvo, Guillermo, Leonardo Leiderman and Carmen M. Reinhart (1993): "Capital Inflows and Real Exchange Rate Appreciation in Latin America: The Role of External Factors". *IMF Staff Papers*, Vol. 40.

Cantor, Richard and Frank Packer (1996): "Determinants and Impact of Sovereign Credit Ratings". Federal Reserve Bank of New York *Economic Policy Review* (September).

Clark, John (1994): "The Structure, Growth, and Recent Performance of the Latin American Bond Market". Federal Reserve Bank of New York, *Research Paper* No. 9416.

Cline, William R and Kevin J S Barnes (1997): "Spreads and Risk in Emerging Markets Lending". Institute of International Finance, *IIF Research Papers* No. 97-1.

Demirgüç-Kunt, Asli and Enrica Detragiache (1994): "Interest rates, official lending, and the debt crisis: A reassessment". *Journal of Development Economics*, Vol. 44, pp. 263-85.

Duffee, Gregory R (1996): "The Variation of Default Risk with Treasury Yields", in Board of Governors of the Federal Reserve System, *Risk Measurement and Systemic Risk*.

Edwards, Sebastian (1984): "*LDC* Foreign Borrowing and Default Risk: An Empirical Investigation, 1976-80". *American Economic Review*, Vol. 74, pp. 726-34.

Edwards, Sebastian (1986): "The Pricing of Bonds and Bank Loans in International Markets: An Empirical Analysis of Developing Countries' Foreign Borrowing". *European Economic Review*, Vol. 30, pp. 565-89.

Eichengreen, Barry and Ashoka Mody (1998a): "What Explains Changing Spreads on Emerging-Market Debt: Fundamentals or Market Sentiment?" *NBER Working Paper* No. 6408, February.

Eichengreen, Barry and Ashoka Mody (1998b): "Interest Rates in the North and Capital Flows to the South: Is There a Missing Link?" *International Finance*, Vol. 1, No. 1, pp. 35-57.

Feder, Gershon and Knud Ross (1982): "Risk Assessments and Risk Premiums in the Eurodollar Market". *Journal of Finance*, Vol. 37, pp. 679-91.

Fons, Jerome S (1994): "Using Default Rates to Model the Term Structure of Credit Risk". *Financial Analysts Journal*, Vol. 50, pp. 25-32.

Helwege, Jean and Christopher M Turner (1996): "The Slope of the Credit Yield Curve for Speculative-Grade Issuers". *Mimeo*, Federal Reserve Bank of New York.

International Monetary Fund (1997): *International Capital Markets: Developments, Prospects, and Key Policy Issues*. Washington, D.C.

Larrain, Guillermo, Helmut Reisen and Julia von Maltzan (1997): "Emerging Market Risk and Sovereign Credit Ratings". OECD Development Centre, *Technical Papers* No. 124.

Min, Hong G. (1998): "Determinants of Emerging Market Bons Spread - Do Economic Fundamentals Matter?" The World Bank, *Policy Research Paper* No. 1899.

Özler, Sule (1992): "The evolution of credit terms: An empirical study of commercial bank lending to developing countries". *Journal of Development Economics*, Vol. 38, pp. 79-97.

Rockerbie, Duane W (1993): "Explaining interest spreads on sovereign Eurodollar loans: *LDC*s versus *DC*s, 1978-84". *Applied Economics*, Vol. 25, pp. 609-16.

www.ingramcontent.com/pod-product-compliance
Lightning Source LLC
Chambersburg PA
CBHW081801170526
45167CB00008B/3272